SINE QUA NON

haiku and tanka

Elliot Nicely

SINE QUA NON

ISBN 978-1-958408-44-5

Red Moon Press
PO Box 2461
Winchester VA
22604-1661 USA
www.redmoonpress.com

Cover image: *Winter Thaw*
Unknown, 20th century.
Oil on canvas, 22.5" x 24.25".
Private collection of the author.
Used with Permission

Author Photo: Asa Nicely

first printing

For my sons

Asa *&* **Eli**

my Alpha and Omega

SINE QUA NON

NATURA

where words fail pines along the cliff's edge

scent of rain
a starless wind stirs
last year's leaves

wisps of fog
gathering morning light
a steelhead rises

neighborhood gossip
from blossom to blossom
honey bees

dandelion field
the summer wind casts
a thousand wishes

abandoned greenhouse
inside and out
wildflowers

too much moonshine the echo of bullfrogs

midsummer storm
all the ways
the willow bends

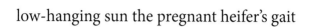

low-hanging sun the pregnant heifer's gait

darkness edges in
the shades of purple
in the killdeer's call

deeper into dusk
along the railroad tracks
ripe elderberries

late supper
the crisscrossing of bats
beneath the barn light

quarry lake:
a ghost tree rises
out of the moon

veterans' day the geese adjust their formation

escaping steam
from the field-dressed deer —
deep autumn

deep autumn
a bare maple
cradles the sunset
even now, the weight
of that word *infertile*

blue-black cold . . .
this low wind within
the pine barrens

in the crook
of the no vacancy sign
cold sparrows

the stillness
of the porch swing
winter rain

TEMPUS

new year's day the times square street sweeper

slow to be seated
— a fountain koi
spits up a pebble

waxing gibbous
the diner specials the same
as yesterday

first touch of gray—
the weathered clapboard
of a distant barn

older now . . .
the edges
of dawn
vanishing into
the ground fog

afternoon drizzle . . .
at the British Museum
a whale-bone chess set

dawn-lit horizon
the sandstone cliffs
the shape of the wind

buck moon
rubbing away the velvet
from my own antlers

on her path
to womanhood . . .
queen anne's lace

late summer drizzle
the sidewalk chalk drawings
fade

first day of school the droop of sunflowers

autumn migration
the pull of my son's hand
from mine

empty sandlot
a shadow slides
across home plate

father's advice
. . . the faded blue
of his ball cap

the last time we spoke the tangled shadows of telephone wires

between
the question and answer . . .
rain-swept moon

storm waves
through the winter wheat
how wrong I've been

what would have been
our anniversary
scent of snow

winter solstice the length of a windowsill

below zero
for the third day
the lowing of bulls

no matter
this broken clock . . .
pulsing stars

flowering bittersweet . . .
the chances
i did take

DEUS

Epiphany

rearranging

this

emptiness

Good Friday
gravity swallows the light
from a dying star

copper-streaked cheeks
The Blessed Virgin
cupping rain

the months since
my last confession . . .
browning lilacs

asking one more time . . .
the breadth
of a prairie dawn

the day after
her first communion —
cicada shells

all the shades of red
throughout the church glass
all saints' day

all souls' day
frost blankets
the potter's field

christmas morning
ladders of sunlight rise
from the empty pews
throughout the church
the scent of frankincense

winter constellations
all these roads again
leading home

MORS

the groundhog's shadow
white where there shouldn't be
on her mammogram

waiting
for her lab results —
the black between stars

in the icu
a ventilator's slow exhale . . .
winter deepens

the sprint of gulls
along the shoreline
more dark news

hospice unit:
all these settings
on the dimmer switch

alzheimer's patient . . .
a familiar creak
from the rocking chair

first prayer
of the wake
only the wine breathes

blackberry winter
in the cemetery
a fresh grave

church graveyard
a granite vase
brimming with rain

survivor's guilt
the rain-faded yellows
of this ribbon

the lapping
of an empty clothesline
estate sale

rain-soaked newspaper
no mention of our neighbor
lost to the war

AMOR

sun-lit snow the brush of her skirt

early spring
the pink tips of emerging
magnolia blossoms —
twisting the end
of her lipstick

first date
no fortune cookies
with the bill

newly shaven legs
steam rises
from the wet asphalt

summer solstice the distance to her lips

front porch dusk
we linger a moment
in our goodnights
the reach of my shadow
the breadth of her smile

second kiss
— a quickening
of passing railcars

new love . . .
offering the firefly
cupped in my hands

getting tipsy
in our underwear —
adolescent moon

skinny dipping
the pull of the moon
in your voice

asking about
past lovers —
closed morning glories

all the wrong words vine-wrapped fence

heat lightning
— my silence
answers hers

marriage counseling —
an unexpected wind shifts
the burn barrel smoke

that which is unsaid
— condensation
streaks the window

her eyes
avoid my apology
false spring

red maple buds —
how long since
we've made love?

to forgive again no moon only stars

cold snap
she resumes correcting
my crossword

newly separated —
she adds a hyphen
between our last names

the way
she says goodbye
this time
the sunset refills
her wine glass

divorce papers —
the suddenness
of sparrows

what might have been . . .
our shadows become one
then part

ACKNOWLEDGMENTS

Thank you to the editors of the following publications in which some of these poems, or earlier versions of these poems, first appeared:

Acorn — "all the wrong words" (#24), "blackberry winter" (#33), "winter constellations" (#37), "flowering bittersweet" (#38), "father's advice" (#41), "church graveyard" (#51).

Atlas Poetica — "early spring" (#6).

bottle rockets — "dandelion field" (#16), "abandoned greenhouse" (#20), "summer solstice (#21), "late summer drizzle" (#22), "to forgive again" (#24), "winter solstice" (#24), "storm waves" (#28), "veterans' day" (#35), "newly separated" (#36), "front porch dusk" (#41), "Epiphany" (#47), "hospice unit" (#50).

Eucalypt — "the way" (#20), "christmas morning" (#21), older now (#23).

Frogpond — "waiting" (33.2), "the last time" (35.3), "skinny dipping" (40.1), "autumn migration" (40.2), "escaping steam" (41.2), "midsummer storm" (43.3), "no matter" (46.1), "quarry lake" (46.3).

Kernels — "late supper" (1.1).

Kingfisher — "asking one more time" (#2).

Kokako — "newly shaven legs" (#9), "asking about" (#9), "where words fail" (#22), "on her path" (#27), "getting tipsy" (#29), "blue-black cold" (#30), "divorce papers" (#30).

Mayfly — "copper-streaked cheeks" (#41).

Modern Haiku — "below zero" (41.3), "her eyes" (43.1), "first day of school" (44.1), "what would have been" (45.2), "the groundhog's shadow" (47.2), "sun-lit snow" (47.3), "the sprint of gulls" (47.3), "all the shades of red" (48.3), "darkness edges in" (49.1), "all souls' day" (49.2), "new year's day" (54.3), "afternoon drizzle" (55.1).

Moonset — "slow to be seated" (2.2), "the day after" (3.1), "neighborhood gossip" (4.1), "too much moonshine" (5.1), "that which is unsaid" (6.1).

Nisqually Delta Review — "wisps of fog" (3.1).

Notes from the Gean — "what might have been" (3.2), "rain-soaked newspaper" (3.4).

Paper Wasp — "first touch of gray" (14.3).

Presence — "browning lilacs" (#56), "between" (#59), "empty sandlot" (#61), "cold snap" (#63), "scent of rain" (#64), "survivor's guilt" (#64), "in the icu" (#66), "deep autumn" (#68), "the stillness" (#68), "low-hanging sun" (#74), "waxing gibbous" (#77), "deeper into dusk" (#79).

Riverbed Haiku — "the lapping" (#3).

The Seasons of Haiku Trail (Kirtland, Ohio) — "new love" (2018).

White Lotus — "first date" (#4), "alzheimer's patient" (#6), "heat lightning" (#6), "marriage counseling" (#7), "the second kiss" (#7), "in the crook" (#7), "first prayer" (#8), "red maple buds" (#9).

I also want to extend my thanks to Thomas Haynes, Bryan Rickert, and Tom Sacramona who provided me with invaluable feedback on early drafts of my manuscripts as well as express my eternal gratitude to the staff of the Lakewood Public Library.

ELLIOT NICELY is a secondary school teacher and the author of three haiku chapbooks — most recently *Weathered Clapboard* (2023). He served on the Haiku North America 2023 Programming Committee in addition to having served as a judge for the Haiku Society of America's 2024 Merit Book Awards. He resides in Lakewood, Ohio. *Sine Qua Non* is his first full-length collection of poetry.